# Greetings from Guilka, Ballymoe:

*Poems from the Head and the Heart*

by

William Tiernan

First Published in 2016 by The Manuscript Publisher

ISBN: 978-0-9576729-6-3

A CIP Catalogue record for this book is available from the National Library

Typesetting, page design and layout, cover design by DocumentsandManuscripts.com

Cover illustration: *Breaking the Darkness* by Anne Rigney

# *Greetings from Guilka, Ballymoe:*
## *Poems from the Head and the Heart*

# Dedication

I dedicate this book of poems to my late, loving parents, John Joe and Celia, and also, my brother, Michael, whom I miss dearly to this day. I also dedicate it to Little Shane and Michael James and to Big Lal too, and to all the great people of this parish who have travelled on.

# Foreword

I was there in a wide open field, a young boy with flowing curly hair. My father and my siblings were in fields of green stalks and golden-coloured corn. I felt so alive and free, saying to myself, 'Take a look at the face of the wide open space when you're feeling down.'

Indeed, I just loved the coloured greenery of life. What the Earth had to offer. Why the Earth had so many beautiful things. Willie and Mattie and Jimmy and Christy, Yvonne, Kitty, Nora, Sis, Michael, Joe and Maggie – all beautiful neighbours with innocent minds and hard-working hands. Those who lived of the land accepted their crosses without stress. They had great devotion to their religion and their great acts of kindness and Christianity, while harbouring their fear of the priest but I won't go any further than that. That was my village of Guilka. With the way I write about it, you'd feel you'd want to be there.

I owe so much to my parents, for all they did for me down through the years, especially my mother. She didn't have it easy. The work was hard but we took no notice of it whatsoever. In fact, we enjoyed it.

I didn't like schools, in fact I hated it. 'Please Sir and please Miss,' you'd say with your hand up, like a little beggar. Secondary school wasn't any better: you got trounced as usual, though, I have to say, I was never beaten in school. Thankfully, I was never beaten out of it either. The first three years, I attended an all-boys school, which was a terrible idea. I started and ended my last two years of education in a mixed school. Up to that point, I had never thought about girls. At first, I was shy around girls – a bit like a choir boy in a brothel. I overcame that shyness quite quickly and began to really love women and to this day, I adore women. They are all beautiful and interesting. They think differently than we men think and that's not one bit of harm.

However, the darkness was spinning in and out of my life, which was uncomfortable at the time. In fact, it was uncomfortable most of my young life and older life. Winston Churchill coined it well – The Black Dog he called his mental illness. Today we call it depression, without shame or fear. My relationship with women, I found difficult because of my dark periods and mood swings. It was made hard by the calculated sounds of hissing anger and psychological ticks. While I was always aware that there was nothing wrong with me, I always felt there was something not right. Possessiveness, panic attacks, wanting to withdraw from the world: I had it all.

Anyway, I want to drift away from my dark periods to the future that lies ahead, though I know the future will always be the present. We all have our plans and dreams but, no matter how far our imagination takes us, or how far transport can take us, we will always remain in the present. Some might find that hard to understand. A lovely friend of mine, who was a psychologist, enticed me into writing poetry. She said to me, "Willie, you have an eye of a poet."

Well afterwards, thinking to myself of how I had wanted to start writing for some time, I began to write and the rest is history.

The Black Dog of depression became the bleak dog and he became even blacker, until I fell into a deep despair and had to accept hospitalization. For three years, I was severely depressed. It was not bi-polar but uni-polar depression that I was diagnosed with: a condition that means that you're depressed all the time. I wore a mask for the world. All I can say is that I am at a very peaceful place in life now. I've won first prize nationally for writing a poem about my late brother Michael[1], whom I miss to this day as well as my mother. I miss both of them and always will. My brother died shortly after my mother. She sent for him and both are now in a better place.

We must never forget that we are all loved unconditionally by God. Forget the word 'purity' as it does not exist on this planet. It never did and never will. We learn to release ourselves from fear of God;

---

[1] *My Brother Michael* by William Tiernan (included in this volume – see page 1) was awarded the National Winner prize in the poetry category at the Hanna Greally Literary Awards 2014, organised as part of the SiarScéal Festival that takes place in Roscommon every year.

from the rubbish we've been fed. This rubbish has not just been fed to us down through the years but down through the centuries, by men who were as straight as a straight answer out of Dáil Éireann. God is all-loving, forgiving and is the supreme. There is no such thing as eternal damnation. God does not create and then eternally damn. This would be a failure and in Creation, there is no failure. We must bring everybody along with us. Love and mercy must come out of all of our lives. Without this and God, there is no life. At the moment, things are pretty scary. The migrants, Russia, America and China – I feel we may be on the verge of chaos. I was going to say hunger and war but we already have both. We cannot put our faith in humanity. Governments speak and act with their minds and not their hearts. There will never be world peace.

And believe me when I say, there is no melancholy running through me as I write this, not anymore. I am blessed to have such wonderful brothers and sisters. They encourage me constantly. When I came first nationally for my poem, my sister, Catherine, came all the way up from Cork, stopping in Galway to collect my sister, Eileen, before heading down home to see me. I am eternally grateful for them all. I am also blessed with some lovely lady friends – Mary D, Mary C, Una, Anne, Teresa, Eithne, Collette, Nora, and Eileen G.

When I wanted to get a book published, I asked three lovely ladies if they would help me. They immediately jumped to my assistance. I told them I wanted no money out of it. I do not write for money and never will.

*When we look out in wonder*
*At all the diamond stars,*
*We see life as so far;*
*We must not forget who we are.*


To all my lovely lady friends, I thank the three of you for helping me to fulfil my dream and get some of my work out there. Anne, Eithne and Teresa, you are the salt of the earth: the same earth that mothers us all.

Would I like to get married I wonder, if I would like a woman living with me? I am so set in my ways. I love the silence, I embrace it. I can come and go as I like. They say, when you get old, you will have no one to look after you. Those who say that speak out of insecurity and lack of faith. We are all looked after; no one is ever alone. Who knows what the future will bring? I don't know and neither does anyone else. How fortunate we should feel!

I hope you can all enjoy the poems. As for home ... let your hearts be your home: mine is. In my world, there is no tomorrow, or future for I live in the now. Just because we put our own shoes on in the morning, does not mean someone else will be taking them off in the evening!

Look out everyone.

God bless and take care,

*William Tiernan*
*4 November 2015*

# About the Author

William Tiernan is a Galway-based poet and author. His writings reflect his personal experiences and convictions, as well as strong ties to the community in which he lives, his identification with the place where he grew up.

He has been writing for a number of years and has brought together a selection of his poem, for the first time, in this volume entitled, *Greetings from Guilka, Ballymoe: Poems from the Head and the Heart.*

His poem, *My Brother Michael,* included here, was judged National Winner in the poetry category at the Hanna Greally Literary Awards in 2014.

# Contents

# My Brother Michael

You had holes in your life
But never in your heart,
Despite the terrible darkness,
That tore your life apart.

We were crushed by the darkness,
Standing on that broken hill.
Others, like us, too were crushed,
All of us coming away unfulfilled.
All of us coming away, wishing our rivers be still.

I won't be coming out to play anymore;
Your eyes have been closed forever more.
The chapter of life closed and your world has shut its door.
We were the heart and the blood.
We crossed barbed wire and walked through mud.
Mother's distant dinner time call.
Oh, the simplicity of it all!
I look for you in the heavens or on some shiny star,
As I mingle through my own life and look out through its bars.
We were herding and feeding sheep and cattle:
It was part and package of the battle.
Mornings we'd rise to the call of the corncrake,
Helping Daddy make hay with the horse and rake.
I see us in fields of honey-coloured corn,
Of thistles and of thorns,
Bending over with mother gathering sheaves
And the music of the wind rustling through the trees.

Our world would stop and start again at the name of something
    new,
And in its outpouring of grief and pain,

The gods of the truth always come true.
On the quiet by-road, without burden or load

Our conversation goes back to a simpler way,
When our feet danced so excitedly.,
Above the warmth of the clay.
I know we can't be forever of body and mind
But the footsteps of our departure must rhyme.

Young male savages experiencing life on its tracks.
Smoking fags behind our parents' backs.
I'm sorry about the girlfriend you never got to love.
I'm sorry about all the crimes against the moon above.
All the parts of our lives where love and dust concealed
And all the other people, whose layers in life have yet to be
    peeled.

It was so hard for you to succeed when the battle of life failed to
    understand your need ...
I could see the dying in your eyes
But I see them marvel at the skies.
I find it so hard to believe you are dead;
I have so many pictures of you in my head.

I loved your sense of humour and smile;
You carried it with you through your own inner child.
Sometimes, I feel I can hear yours and mother's voices carried in
    the wind,
When I feel that time is healing and I'm on the mend.
I look back at our lives in days of yore
And I look and see you and mother no more.

Illustration used courtesy of **Anne Rigney**

# Guilka, 1990

Guilka, oh my Guilka!
Shall we sigh and say ah?
Your fresh green fields of life
Saw days of struggle and strife.
Days when gangs would sit and talk
And new-born babies learned to walk.
Where old men smoked their pipes in peace
And women dried their clothes in the breeze.
Dogs barked and cats growled,
And lambs were threatened as the fox howled.

Where Christy's was the only car
And they said Cathy would become a star.
Where blackberries were picked by the roadside
And the thrill of stealing auld Joe's bike.
The old ass and cart, and horse and trap,
And Miko's baldhead always covered with a cap.
Where in your island river, we used to swim,
And Shuffler – will we ever forget him?

Guilka; with the sunlight shining on your stream
And Seaneen's jokes were such a scream,
Flowing gently down from Lisnageerah Hill,
Always running – never still.
And Mauty's jennet with a load of turf,
His dog beside him, barking wurf.
As kids we sat on its shaft and upset its load;
I can still hear him cursing us from the middle of the road.

Guilka, Guilka! A short cut across the Curragh,
Scamper children off and hurrah.
Guilka; watching her children going to school,

And try to knock the price of sweets from some auld fool.
Where turf was turned and hay was saved;
Men came home blind drunk and raved.
Where stories were told around the fire.
Exaggerated tales grew higher and higher.
The postman always delivered the envelope,
With dollars and pounds – always giving hope!
Where a neighbour was a neighbour and a friend a friend:
Rows sometimes, but we always made up again.

Where September brought the thrashing machine;
The women cooked and kept the home clean.
A many a winter's snow you turned
But summer days always returned.
Oh, Guilka, now you're standing frozen and still,
Though the stream still flows down from the hill.
Your shutters are all nailed,
Your memories jailed.

Your windows broke and walls cracked.
Not a sound of an ass and cart,
No smoke rising from your chimney tops.
You watched your old get old and go,
You watched your young grow and flow.
Flow from your narrow, winding boreens:
Many of them never to be seen again.

Guilka; whistling to the sound of a haunted breeze.
All your children gone across the seas.
Your carpets are now all covered in dust,
Your gates and padlocks are all gone to rust.
Your barns have now all caved in.
The river still flows without a soul to swim.
Guilka, oh how you bleed!
Oh, how I understand your need.

You crave for faces to come through.
No faces come, nothing new.

The dead are buried and gone forever;
The young are gone, never to be together.
Guilka; your trees losing their leaves to the ground,
Winter is coming, so will summer but without a sound.
Guilka – my tiny little village!
From your lonely eyes comes a spillage.
Tears for your children who used to play;
Those you loved who had to stray.
Guilka; one of many tiny veins without its blood,
Sucked, dried and drained of all that was once good.

Illustration used courtesy of **Eamon Hayden**

# The Weekend

My weekend was quiet.
It was light when it was day
And quiet when it was night.

The morning spoke so softly;
The rain has been soft and light.
There is a glint of light left
Under the western sky
But very soon, it will die.

I'm following a chasing smile:
The inner twin vision of my inner child.
The poems written by running streams,
The gods of higher dreams.

Ever since I lost my youth,
I've searched outside and inside
For spiritual truth.
Sometimes, from God's spoken breath,
There can come love;
There can come death.

Illustration used courtesy of **Anne Rigney**

# Poem of Longing

In my darkest hour,
I see you as a flower
Blossoming and blooming into beauty.
Groomed and shaped so shapely,
The blessed light bulbs burning,
As the pages of your eyes are turning.
Your hair curled like a wave flowing.
Your face lit like a lamp burning.

I'm a stranger tramp to your body and mind:
I feel sacrificed by your unworthy time.
In shadows and in waters ledge,
I hang out on the edge,
My wounds hurt from loneliness,
My depressed mind wounded by unhappiness.

Frail as I am to pretend
And weak as I am to lend,
The firepower of a heart's blood,
To be born again into the body of God.

Illustration used courtesy of **Anne Marie Finan**

# Thanks to St. Dympna

In my lifelessness and darkest despair,
Sitting on a thorn waiting to repair
Years built of out of desperate hours.
A cracked wall bursting open, a yellow flower,
The black lock and key of the tower.
Once a place for every 'Black Dog' prisoner,
Who had to take their broken self-esteem off at the door,
Their only friend, their shadow on the shaky floor.
To heal and to hurt again.
To hurt again and wait to heal again.

Meet me where they play the blues
And I'll bring you back some dark, heavy news.
If we're learning as the fires of hell are burning,
Are we healing with every new season that's turning?
With every raw nerve and stomach churning,
Every wild black dart that's thrown in the night, yearning.
With every dart so wild and free,
They pierce your confidence chord.
All these complex characters within to let me be,
Like I'm starving out of some kind of mystery.

As I come before my Lord,
On Judgement Day, I'll fall upon the Earth
And cry, "My Lord, there are far worse things than death."
Pushed and punched against the walls of our decay,
From the budding power of our own childish passion play,
Borrowed and still stolen that was once footprints of our
    stairways.
Oh, Heaven's gate be closed!
Oh, Heaven's gate be open!
Our thickest skin has cracked and forever broken.

I have waited on Captain Blackness for so long,
That used to whisper into my listening ear,
And startle me with their lyrics, I didn't have to fear.

Their voices echo from history's dead page
A meaningless imagery, uncontrolled rage.
Too many blockages in the flowing red tide of our veins,
Alongside Freud and Jung, caught without an umbrella in the
    rain.
But we can dream of falling into our dead lovers' arms:
Who spent their whole lives wrestling with the storm;
Whose serpent had to crawl across the desert and forced to eat
    sand,
Choked before the stigmata of our saint's hands.

So hold, all you pretty young ones!
The Darkness is only to see the day is done
And in our togetherness, we know God is one.
Our new day has begun without water or sun.
Only a day to take us back into the hour,
Where they will give us old clothes at the temple.

Knowing, by now, that our world is never simple,
The crust of loaf that got stabbed and burst,
In this long drawn out corridor, our symptoms they just got
    worse.
All the drained creatures have all been pulled along the river,
Thrown out of the savage sea,
Survivals rough edge head, turning, making my hairs shiver.

Oh Mother, my kind heavenly angel!
I'm sorry for what I put you through:
When I was dark, you saw the darkness too.
"It will all pass over," you would say,
For every breath of your ninety years.

My Black Dog belched suicide ideations for clay,
Mother, I would have left you even in the heaven with tears.
Days when I was too weak to leave my bed,
The hungry haunts swirling about my head.
Mother, you were there for me with your rosy cheeks,
From moments that made up the days and weeks.
No Hell for me and you, mother, after all of this.
I felt I was fired against Satan's fiery stench of kiss.

Swallowed I've been, in those false promises where they tie a
  squeal.
The tired rubbing bones and feelings too numb to feel.
When my heart got dark, my life lost all meaning;
All I could do was just keep on dreaming.
I could become a dawn the sun might need,
Instead of becoming a half-warm corpse whose veins have
  started to bleed.
St. Dympna, my friend, holds healing in her hair.
She came to me in a vision in my darkest despair.
She is a beacon of light that can never be quenched;
From her hands and heart, nothing can be wrenched.
In the hardness of this warm touch,
You are being comforted;
They are giving you a crutch.
You'll no longer feel the sadness in the tears of your eyes.
To choose the pages of blackness – you'd rather die!
And your dreamy streets of peace were all a lie.

But we have not come here to live, or to die but to float.
Bringing it all back home, dressed in our warm coats.
The vagabonds are all standing in a line.
They bring you dark thoughts of the mind
But we are all greater than that now;
We will go out with the wheel and the plough.
Time will go backwards but not the sacred cow.

We are there and are in there,
Despite the sorrow and despair.

St. Dympna, I will pick flowers for you
And you will say to God, "Let him come through."

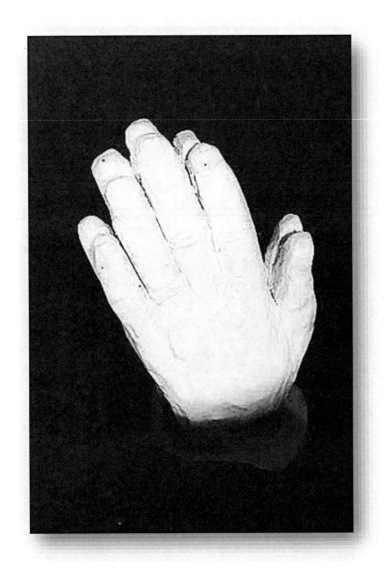

Illustration used courtesy of **Graham Singleton**

# Reflections on Martina

Oh, the lovely sky, from her shins to her thigh
With the pupils so blue,
And the sky too.
Oh, the lovely skirt,
The phoney flirt!

At the wrinkled skin,
At a tight wear in,
The smile angled and painted,
The view senile, having fainted
Into frozen unsympathetic dust and tears,
Worn out by worry and fear.
All that talk and matter is money;
And all that tastes sweet is only honey,

The net is a press button game:
It never has to end in shame,
Only to capitalize and seize the corrupt prize
Against the wrinkled skin,
And every expression it holds and hides within.

Illustration used courtesy of **Anthony Bruen**

# My Darkest Hour

Coming round to my darkest hour,
I peddle the pushing flower,
Without remorse or substance,
Without care or even a pretence glance.
One last salute at farewell;
One last shot out of my broken shell.
This blood inside me warms my marrow veins.
Along the track of life, I try to hang on to the reins.
I've never felt like this before:
Crippled inside and fixated at my shadow on the floor.
Silhouetted by the dust shafts of my inward self;
Standing with lights at a broken door.
Every time my back turns,
The light of my life burns
Until the glow becomes thin and narrow –
I may not be here tomorrow.

Illustration used courtesy of **Eamon Hayden**

# Loving and Losing

The seasons stop and then they start,
With their coming of something new.
Fleeting memories gathering in the heart
And becoming treasures, and memories of you.

Oh, take us from this brokenness,
That the winds of change will come
And both sides will freely run
Into the belly of acceptance and happiness.

I have come to understand
That everyone is numbered,
Just like every grain of sand.
The horses have run and time will always be young.

Here are the wolves and here is our birth,
Here is our life and here is our death.
I like to write little poems and rhymes
To give faith and hope to our hearts and minds.
Forever losing our friends and lovers,
Forever losing our fathers and mothers.

There is a longing in the branches.
There is a longing in the trees.
There is a longing in you and me.
There is a longing in the seas.

Oh, crown of light, oh crown of thorns,
It's only like yesterday that we were all born.
It's our innermost decisions that we delay
But truth and innocence find its way.

Sometimes, we feel we hear your heavenly call
But most time, we leave it be to the mystery of it all.
It's out of love we must all move on
And out of compassion we find our true song.

We are, forever, searching for you in our eyes
But one day, we will see them all
Underneath God's mushroom-coloured, open shawl,
Somewhere in the skies.

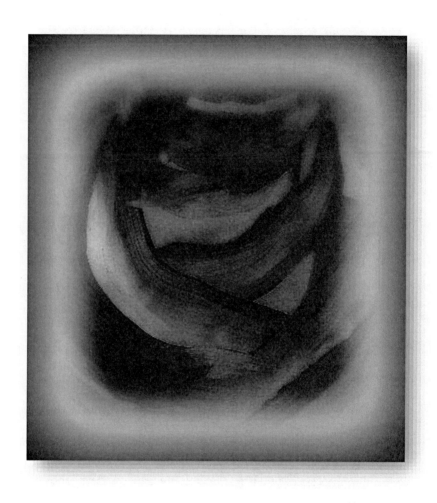

Illustration used courtesy of **Anthony Bruen**

# The Bard of Williamstown

### Ode to My Friend & Poet, Tom Scally

An Cruchain Rua stands so still
And by its side, its furry hill.
The wind whistles ghostly through the flaggers and the rush,
And the birds sprout a lonely tune from a graveyard bush.
How you loved your little village where the heathery breezes
    blow,
The changing of the seasons, from sunshine, wind and snow.
You wrote of all our patriots that made this land so free,
Gave hope to all our immigrants, far across the sea.
You used to love to watch the evening sunset,
Melting in your soul
And loved your native colour of the green, white and gold.
How well you would remember the old times,
There were of times so hard
And you were proud to be from Williamstown,
And proud to be their bard.
You never became addicted to machinery or greed.
You were happy in your De Valera's Ireland;
You had no need.
You loved to grace your home place in the early morning dew:
From the cot where you were born into, you remained forever
    true.
You were a gentleman, poet and friend,
And memories of you will stay with me until my days' end.
I watched you suffering in agony and pain
But never did I once hear you complain.
But cherishing memories of footsteps
Strolling on soft feathery grass,
Or a quiet glass of porter after Sunday morning Mass.
Listening to the cuckoo's call, or the thrush, or the linnet

Sing sweetly in nature's music hall.
Watch the noneens and the buttercups bloom
And read about Tone and Emmett, from the quietness of your
    room.
Those men in their suits are discarding old for new
But they cannot steal you, spirit of Carnderry
Near that hill of Cruchain Rua.
For a dying fire has its ash and it also has its flame,
And power can become powerless between the wicked and the
    lame.
Across those furry hills that's known as Cruchain Rua
Your footsteps will no longer roam,
For the gates of heaven have opened through
To carry your tired spirit home.

Illustration used courtesy of **Graham Singleton**

# Michael

There are many people in your life
And there are many yet to be,
And since you are now under Heaven's light,
There is so much joy you have yet to see.
Yours was a sadness that could never be reached:
A void unbreached.

Fifty-two years you came to slip your skin
For a newer and more colourful world within.
When Heaven's Gates were opening to you,
Your loving mother was coming through
And if ever there was a breath she drew,
That breath would have been unto you.
Everything in life that is sacred,
Everything in life that is broken,
The universe has swallowed home your last human call,
To the other side of the mystery of it all.

In life, they say, time don't give you time.
The beauty of language doesn't always rhyme.
We've seen your eyes open and cry,
We've seen your eyes open and die,
We've seen your Guardian Angel fly
Across the sacred, illuminated sky.
Your physical form is now a sound of heavenly delight
And God's fingerprints on all things, beautiful and bright.

Illustration used courtesy of **Eamon Hayden**

# Poem of Hope

How many happy people are there,
Whose happiness has had to change?
How many times in our lifetime,
Does a lifetime sound so strange?
So many years they have come
To slip pit of their bones
And leaves us with an eerie silence
That gathers around our homes.
Gathering of journeys past
And memories gone to show they really care,
Through dark and light, hard graft and despair.
Remember how it was when we were young:
Our youth could fly so high.
Someday, we will meet them all
Underneath God's mushroom-coloured, open shawl,
Somewhere in the sky.
So step outside of our inner selves
From all despair and gloom,
While the summertime of all our lives
Is still in bloom.

Illustration used courtesy of **Eamon Hayden**

# On the Death of a Baby

Little child, we see you with a smile on your face.
Remembering your presence was filled with grace,
We would have liked to have watched you on a swing,
Playing with other children, circling in a ring.

Take you for a stroll through the feathery grass.
Listen to you bawl out loud at Sunday mass.
Come to see a movie, or maybe a football game.
Come away a player, limping or be lame.

Walking with your uncle, looking after cattle and sheep.
Be put to sleep by fairy-tale stories, like Little Bo Peep.
Take the imaginary monster out of your tiny head
And lay you down securely in your bed.

Let your hair grow and wear around your forehead, a headband.
Take you across the street by holding on to your hand.
Yes, those many games we would have liked to see you play;
Those many urgent words you'd want to say.

It was not God that stole you away
From the brightness of our day.
No one is to bless and no one is to blame,
And no words can ease an eternal pain.

We thank God for the joy you gave us, the short time you were
    here.
In a world full of steel eyes, death and fear;
In many lands where the gun is the promise of salvation,
Instead, it is of destruction and starvation.

Our little baby boy child, you do not sail these shores alone,
For these mountains filled with lost sheep, are made of more
   than stone.
They scrape across the diamond-coloured sky,
Emptying themselves so that one-day, they too can die.

Lost Angel of the Earth to fly
Beyond the fair side of the sun's bye and bye.
While watching burning bridges that we all could have crossed,
We feel close to everyone we've lost.

Times when our hearts should be full of the joy of song,
We find it hard to believe you've really gone.
Now we must painfully put away all your tiny toys
And dream of you in Heaven, with the little girls and boys.

In a world gone frantic in push and rush,
Our hearts are broken and our dreams are crushed.
Watching them lay your tiny, little coffin underground,
Our home without your heartbeat,
Without your sound.

Are you up there with all the angels in song,
Making us feel our existence,
Making us feel we belong?
Memories will hold our tears and all our smiles,
Just before moments at the end of that unbroken mile.

For we cannot change the colour of the dove,
Neither can we change losing the ones we love.
O darling child, this spirit in us, is in you too.
In time, they will collide beyond the horizon of blue.

Illustration used courtesy of **Anne Rigney**

# Reflections on Life

Another winter's snow will turn;
Another summer's sun will burn.
What is it that we've learned,
While behind our backs, the world burned?
What have we learned from the wrongly accused,
From those many who have been emotionally and sexually
    abused?
Those hungry fields of the innocent dispossessed,
The stigmatisation of those who are lonely
Because they are depressed.
Severe social problems go unaddressed.

Women struggle with rearing and bearing children
And, even harder still, to cope with their men.
They've put a few mercenaries on the moon,
All the oceans and seas are being searched for a silver spoon.
Daddy's farm is still growing grass
And they are still puffing powder and hash.
And the stressed out, wine-fuelled housewives still struggle for
    cash:
Children around their feet and a toddler on their laps.

Endless mysteries we will never unravel;
Endless road we have yet to travel.
I could always tell the trees from the wood
And was told that a soul could never be too good.
Time, I feel, reminiscing, I choke
When I think of the loveliest of people disappear like smoke.
There are reasons why bridges are burned and crossed,
A reason why lives are spared and lost.

Talking about the past and best ways we could leave it all
  behind,
And be more certain about the future
And good things we might all find.
Our addictions are bringing us out from under the light,
Into the darkness and out of sight.
Daddy gave me fear and his land,
And Mammy's love and courage, I could understand.

Trying to cope with depression in this divided world of ours.
Time, I feel I could live forever;
Times, only for hours.
Cigarettes are still my friends and crave
Worse ways your road can end.
When will I see you again
If I ever decide to come in from the rain?

Illustration used courtesy of **Graham Singleton**

# Frustration

Last night, she came home and said,
"In this male dominated world of ours, it is so hard to get ahead.
All day long, under sexual distress, I slog like hell,
Come home to our babysitters
And all we hear is yell.
The baby's mouth is innocent but his is not.
Our feelings of frustration are left to rot
On a selfish pocket of drunken release.
I'll go my own way – you do as you please.
Nine months carrying without their understanding of pain,
Yet the smile on your face
Gives you something to gain.
Any comfort or thought at all,
The baby in your arms may say it all."

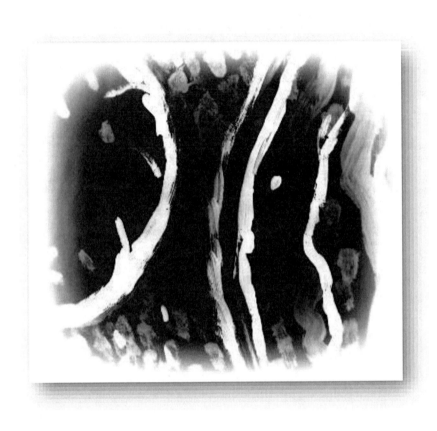

Illustration used courtesy of **Rita Mangan**

# Loneliness

Pot-bellied and thick skin,
Totally weathered within.
Bursting the rough and open door,
That rise to a shiny floor,
Hanging down over its belt,
Not one ounce of emotion it ever felt.

Whiskey in the jar, my love,
To the barmaid pale as a dove.
Bulb nose fractured,
Trousers ruptured.
To explain is but a pain;
To approach would be in vain.

For a creature void of form,
For a sinner out in the storm,
A cheat stranded in his underwear,
A drunk rattled on the tear.

A rat chased by a cat,
A millionaire living in a flat,
The sound of a bear balling,
The voices of rebels calling.

To him, an added weakness:
He has no hunger in his soul,
Nor naked bone to feel the cold
But to maybe quench the light –
The light that makes things bright.

Repressed loneliness has left its stain,
Put beauty back into the picture of pain.

The long journey homeward bound
And all the loved ones he has watched, go to ground.

Illustration used courtesy of **Graham Singleton** and **Eamon Hayden**

## Flight of the Moth

When I was sick in my bed –
The childish hunger haunts in my head –
Then I saw your two great grey-wings spread
And although you are such a little thing,
You caressed the light with your feathery wings,
Towards Heaven's angelic, joyful sound.
Clockwise, you go round and round.
In you, Moth, you dance your own version of universal flight
Into some deep mystery of the night.
It's your floating body that sets you free,
Sets you totally apart from them and me.
You throw great shadows, spinning around the room:
The light bulb between your sun and moon.
I want to tell myself you are nothing,
Yet you are all things created with your body and your wings,
Given to every mystery and to all living things.
For the little spec of time you are here,
You feel neither hurt, nor greed, nor fear:
It is this that sets you free.

Your freedom is never hidden away
In space confined to time.
There is no time, just night and day
But neither have existed in your ghosts of philosophy,
Nor nested in your bed of culture.
You are wild in your body's flight
That's hanging from a piece of web.
This string – your unbroken light –

It sets your body free to form another flight.
Then I got well and left my sickness behind.
Your freedom of flight poured blood into my veins.

I never saw you as a victim of the traps of pain;
Wounded and broken is now your name.
What hurt does ugliness take to kill
The bitter sweetness that still stands
In those haunted hills?
Perhaps, Moth, my body is an apron string
That my soul is hanging from.
I thought, Moth, about new things coming alive
And all delicate things in life could be allowed to survive.

There is no time and there are no years.
The lampshade and the light bulb are your frontiers.

Illustration used courtesy of **Eamon Hayden**

# Shackles of Fear

I'm at rhythm with the stars
And the bars before my eyes,
Skipping lightly beyond the streams
While I open up all my dreams,
Kiss the wind and drink the rain,
Grow fonder of myself
And stand away from pain.

This black line I walk,
I forgive the lot of you.
I never once believed dead ones.
Would it help me come through
If I could have done it on my own?
I would have to have a heart of stone.

So happy for having loved you,
So happy and lucky we didn't come through.
"Stay with me," she says, "for tonight, right here.
Shake off your shackles of Catholicism and fear.
Be by the strength of each other's skin.
Wild out of ourselves with playfulness from within."

"Put it all off for tomorrow," she says.
"What if I've been hurt today?
What if I've been hurt yesterday?
Who sees the tears on the lines of anybody's face?"
The broken innocence that was forced away.
The gods of survival are made of steel:
No poverty or empathy for them to feel,
They cannot.

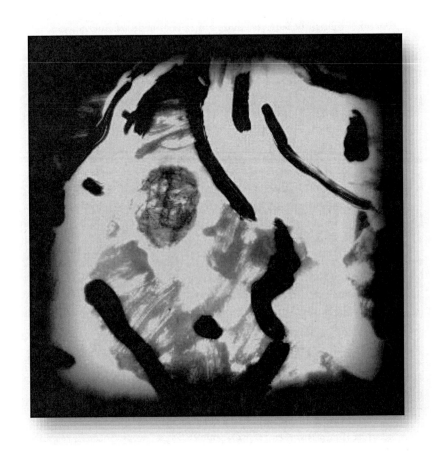

Illustration used courtesy of **Patricia Golden**

# Fine Day

Let the cockerel crow.
Let the sheep and cattle come slow.
Let me be someone unto me
And let the morning be,
On this beautiful fine day.
Let the farmers rejoice and make hay.
Let children lick ice cream from their faces.
Let everyone be in eternal places.
Let them off to a football game;
Let them go to the races.
Let me bathe my eyelids in the morning dew;
Let me prepare for the fine day coming through.
Let no one be a stranger to anyone.
Let the sky rejoice with its loving sun
And on this fine day, may God protect
Each and every one.
Something about a fine day
Makes you feel God's smiles
And helps us get through
Our many crucified miles.
Face the fine day's golden sun
And feel blessed that we are all at one,
Right with our masters, long after the fine day is done.

Illustration used courtesy of **Eamon Hayden**

## Oh Winter

Oh hard winter, you have shut the eye and light of the half day,
As the birds pick at hardship in the clay.
Little children huddled up to one another, off to school to play:
Jack Frost's crunching cold agony.
The one worm wriggles for the one bird only.
Through curtain and bed you call on me,
Whispering over season, river and sea,
Lost, lost, lost, in the valley of frost.
Oh hardship, I have felt the breeze of your ghost.
In the great cathedral, a voice is lost,
Choked, wizened and wintrily frozen,
Robin redbreast and the lifeless wren.
Oh snow; stinging snow, you sting my eyes.
Will I or won't I be ever able rise,
What, with this dead plough on its side?
It won't sow no more; it won't grow no more.
Frozen earth, its limbs you have tore
Out from under costumes that years of sun once wore.
Shut your watery eye and open the other;
She'll be your sister and I'll be your brother,
And the cradle of the heavens holds our mother.
Mother Mary wears a rose as red as blood
And there will be imagined hands, fumbling at a pit of spuds
Where cold shelter throws a narrow glow,
Hungry as an archway in the snow.
Oh sun, oh honey-coloured sun, you may never disappear
But I, now on perished soil, may not have very many years.
Infinity and tap dancing noises in my ears
Of gods and of kings and of mortal men,
Of ice cream hands, of women and children,
Of seconds of moments that now explode.
Our frozen poet tramp with no fixed abode,

His white frosty handkerchief shakes in his feeble hands.
His long, white hair coming down over his face in strands:
Someone should have fed him almost a century ago.
His lines and rhymes, to this day, we'll never know:
He died when I was a warm child by a stone turf fire
But I know, for in his belly, he possessed poetic desire.
Quenched, my perished poetic friend
But I will draw down on them long black lines again.

Illustration used courtesy of **Eamon Hayden**

# Anne the Artist

Off she goes to the USA,
A land where the family is broken,
Or so they say.
Like many a martyr before her,
She'll stretch her body before sunlight
Neath the soft Californian skies.
This artist's eye will open bright
Catching healing colours in her eyes,
Her vision rolling into tattoo land,
Her feet on soft beach sand.
Her artistic ideas and her beautiful, colourful notions
Will bring us all together from this vast and ever flowing ocean.
Flesh and spirit will rise up,
Victorious in art and love.
Footsteps will make their own mark.
The artists will sketch their work.
All dead things will come alive
And all the living, beautiful things will, forever, live.

She will, one day, give the heavens her soul and her heart
But her beauty of earthly vision will live forever in her art.
She radiates such beauty and love
Underneath the sacred light of the heavens above.
While our most vulnerable are struggling with the times,
She has the power to brush hope into their mind.
Nature so strong, yet so delicate
And she can sketch it all with passion and with taste.
Anne, loveen, let your hair hang low
And your water and streams will forever flow.
Beauty and her brush is her gift to the world,
And her honesty, her word.

The Universe will hold her brush and rod.
The Heavens incorporate her into the body of God.

Illustration used courtesy of **Anne Rigney**

# A Sketch of Life

I've never looked at my life as being okay,
Since I have to return to sinders
Or else slowly in life, form decay,
Or tomorrow's today. I could be wearing blinkers,
Be as blind and as beaten as the tinker's ass
And as crooked as the cross I carry to mass,
As it's all full of passion and power
Put into the strain of the word.
As old ones bend to pluck the flower,
Young ways have never heard.
Young years of age they oppress you
And search of guilt and sin.
How on God's earth do you come through,
Learn to love yourself and begin?
In the flames, the cloven-hoofed beast is wild.
On the wool pack clouds, the master is mild.
On the diamond studded highway,
I ride only by chance
And on the dark deep sway,
I'm compelled by a glance.
Send your brat pack brother and sisters;
This day is going to be lonely,
Full of strangers and twisters,
And things that go on and on.
I see myself on a picture of a memorial car.
I think of life so beautiful, phoney and hard.
Is it always Mankind that creates misfortune and mistrust?
Doesn't the eagle fly down and kill the hare
And people born into land lay bare?
I've never looked at my life as being okay;
I've just sketched it out for today.

Illustration used courtesy of **Anne Rigney**

# Negative Attraction

In the still of the night,
Winters perished inch of light,
Fires die out but light never dies,
The heavens open up to the spirit of the sky.
Negative attraction is always drawing near.
The mind thinking shallow and unclear.

The body is broken down, of its energy lost,
That hangs in the gallery of frost.
We died and were reborn of breath,
And mysteriously saved from the experience of death.

Its peace and quiet they all need,
Before they kneel at their troughs to feed.
We're all together, never apart:
We are all light and we are the dark,
Buried in their addictions, running from themselves:
Insecurities concealed by the dust on their shelves.

Brothers, too many of you are dying.
Sisters, so many of you are left alone, pregnant and crying.
All those hearts in love but coming like refugees,
Like a helpless bat tossed upon the seas.

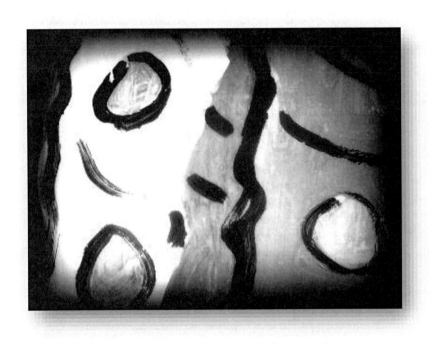

Illustration used courtesy of **Paddy Joe Brennan**

# A Review

I have travelled many journeys drawn with lines,
Written many poems of word and rhymes.
The power that is inside me is in my mind:
An energy that holds me, from the beginning of time.

But my quest for knowledge and wisdom
Will keep me searching,
From its forces, from the outside,
That are always reaching.
It rocked from the cradle in bawls and cries,
And then held in deep inhalation and prying eyes.

I wonder and always wonder
If they were bound in tar and cement,
Or just didn't reach inside lines of journey,
Or were always told to repent.

I have seen all holy pages turning
While flesh and bone were burning,
And though my many line of journey
Will reach a cul-de-sac
And the ones who hold me in deep inhalation,
Will be long laid on their backs.

Before our fences facing
And our thoughts of dying racing,
While white clouds and angry skies,
Have bled open and stormed,
With or without us, the future will be formed.

Through the tunnel of white light,
My journey will draw its last lines

And tomorrow's winds will blow new children,
Drawing energy from their minds.

Illustration used courtesy of **Anthony Bruen**

# Dance Me a Figure

Sketch with me a figure
Slowly like a dream.
Dance with me a figure
To music from a running stream,
Down past the distant shadows
That fall on flakes of skin,
Past the reviews of hypocrites
Who pick up on our breadcrumb sins.
Lives that are sheltered
Against the frame of strain,
On this merry-go-round, well weathered,
Again and again,
Touched by every vision, dressed in silhouettes,
Far from the highway of regrets.
Sketch with me a figure
Underneath the amber moon.
Shape me up with your features
With its image on the silver spoon.
Sparkle with a diamond glow
Your pale face white as snow.
Whispers of wind through light meadows,
Born from the dawn,
Pushing themselves towards the gallant sky.
Sketch me a figure, until the world says goodbye.

Illustration used courtesy of Eamon Hayden

## Kilcroan Cemetery

They are sleeping in Kilcroan;
Never more for the poor devils ever to roam.
They are sleeping in Kilcroan;
Never more to dwell in their own homes.
They are sleeping in Kilcroan;
Gone the clay side from the whitened bone.
Gone the hungry look, paved into stone.

Everybody beside everybody in a place
Where everybody is alone,
Their souls no longer starved,
Their features no longer carved
By our prayer books or our false prophesies.
They were kings and they were queens;
They had their hearts set on their dreams.

It was sad to have to watch them go;
Some went fast, others slow.
They were the summer of all our hearts.
They were the heat that set off our spark.
They chased and struggled with life
And with pleasure.
Always sad to see lovely flowers decay:
Sadder more, to see your loved ones slip away.

Standing in the yard, splitting timber logs,
Loading up the ass and cart for the bog,
Feeding cats and patting their friendly dogs.
When they were young, their blood hot and warm,
Right from the fresh breath of spring,
Right through the eye of the life's every storm.

Fresh their features were, while visible before the stars,
Coming home from school with brown mouths, eating penny
      bars.
Bursting hot tar bubbles on the road
Without the burden or the load.
Times I may be mad and times I may be blind:
Such emotions I feel and must leave behind.
Nobody was ever left stranded and everybody was kind
In this flat Kilcroan, stripped of both body and mind.

All symbols out of dust and mud
Sitting around tables peeling spuds,
Everyone inside themselves, feeling good.
No need for outlaws or Robin Hood:
God's word was the priest's word,
And the priest's word was God's.
Nobody argued, only just giving their approved nods.

Men sitting on high stools, walloping pints of Guinness
And their wives at home with children,
Crying out for food and the price of a new dress.
No one had high expectations and just got along,
Went to Confessions to tell the priests their wrongs,
Came home feeling saved and cleaned up for another while,
Wearing their faces with a big broad smile.
Lucifer wasn't going to get any of them;
Nobody was going to die in sin.

Everybody was badly dressed in their bodies
But purified in their souls.
Got educated in a rat-infested shithole.
I'm sitting in Kilcroan, dressed in body and bone,
Thinking of all the empty houses
And my own silent home.

All the women I chased, yet rarely got the feel.
All the privacy of our lives that became so available to steal.


Every year the missionaries would come
To frighten the shit out of everyone, with Hell's fire and
    damnation
And me so young, thinking God as a love of creation.
The hardship didn't kill them
But it may have supressed their emotions.
Many is the day, they filled both field and bog,
Cutting and catching turf, chasing girls and frogs.
They were good Catholics and God-fearing people
That believed everything they heard from the steeple.


The Prods and every other religion went somewhere else.
They weren't sure where:
Probably gathering cobwebs on some rusty, dusty shelf.
There is an antidote for ignorant persistence
But there's no antidote for empty resistance.
Kilcroan, you hold the ace, the deuce and the jack,
And from where I'm sitting, there's no going back.


Try to conjure up an image of souls
Heading off towards the sky:
Even the most heaviest and hottest hitters in town,
You hold in the all-tightly underground.
And, I'm sure, if we all could make a deal with God,
I'm sure we'd like to have most of them above the sod.
I'm enchanted by all these lovely headstones:
They hold the memory of our loved one's shiny bones.
My God, what warm presence they once held in all our homes.


They are here and they are somewhere else.
I hope to join them, while making that call all by myself.
That call that's taking me a lifetime

And all the challenges of my enquiring mind.
Me and father and mother and brother,
Sitting by our village's running stream
And one day they will open up their doors,
And take me into their dreams.

So many more things I wished to have told them all,
Before the earth drowned out their final call.
Nights without a soulmate and unable to sleep;
There is an angel in my room that dries the tears I weep.
Oh memory, your ghosts serve me, oh, so deep,

Every time I hear the sound
Of the Croan's church bell ring:
The souls on the choir with their hymns,
Coffins head for hearses without hitches,
Women wetting their knickers and men tightening their britches.
We will all swim in the knowledge
Of our gods of clay and stone:
Their sweet and honest conscience of their bone.

Some, when young and others, old –
The Good Lord called them all to his fold.
A new sight and vision of rebirth;
The beginning and the end of death.
A lifetime it took them all before
They were allowed to be free:
Short or long of it, it was meant to be.
Sometimes, it seems a quiet desperation;
Other times, a cruel separation.

I leave them all in the knowledge
That they have become new
And on this, each of which we dwelt upon,
It's left to me and you.

From my little patch of Guilka ground,
I will one day have to leave for
The Kilcroan underground.

Illustration used courtesy of **Anthony Bruen**

# Acknowledgements

Sponsorship received with thanks from the Galway Roscommon Mental Health Services and Mr Michael Fitzmaurice TD.

Appreciation and gratitude is also extended to Eithne Jarrett (EmployAbility, Castlerea), Mary Delaney, Edel Keaveney, Fiona Southwood and Anne Rigney for their invaluable work in co-ordinating this project.

A special thanks to all the artists who have graciously allowed their artwork and photographs to be reproduced in this book.